MY
RAMADAN
PLANNER

ISBN Print: 979-8-59-546269-3
For any inquiries Contact us at notespress@mail.com
© Illustrations, Leaf seamless cover art by Hannah Hattey Dave

This book belongs to:

....

Ramadan the holy month of worship, study of the Quran, prayer, and fasting. Ramadan (the ninth month of the lunar year observed by Muslims) occurs during the month in which Muslims believe the Quran began to be revealed to the Prophet Muhammad (PBUH). It is a joyful celebration for Muslims.

Fasting is one of the Five Pillars of Islam. Healthy adults are expected to observe the fast. (Adults who aren't able to fast, must either pay Fidya or Kaffarah to make up for each missed fast)
During Ramadan, the fast helps believers purify their hearts, renew their faith, seek forgiveness, and increase self-discipline alongside the positive effects on mental wellbeing and spiritual focus. It is also a time to focus on what is most important and positive in a Muslim's life.

The Ramadan fast is absolute. Each day, from the time of Suhoor until Iftar, Muslims abstain from all food and water. Nothing may be consumed during these hours. Believers are also encouraged to ditch bad habits, abstain from anger, and to show compassion.
Fasting really beneficial and can be a way to increase awareness of Allah and to be more aware of the plight of those who are poor and suffering (which is the aim of Ramadan).
Acts of charity are encouraged.
Now that Ramadan is here, we begin to see not through our eyes but through our hearts our spiritual sight increases through the worship of Allah!

This planner is designed to help you Make The Most Out Of this holy month. This book features 2 pages for each day of Ramadan
Plan your day with daily schedule prompts, prayer tracker, Dua of the day, today's goals, and daily habits.
Plan your meals with iftar and suhoor meal plans, to-do list, and a daily reflection section for gratitude and mindfulness.

The main challenge people face during Ramadan is keeping their minds focused. Hunger and lack of sleep can kick in as a distraction.

This journal will help you be productive, perform your daily worship activities, and keep your mind focused. By planning your days carefully, you can focus your time and attention on your plan. The challenge is to keep your momentum going.

Tip 1: schedule things that need high energy during the morning such as meetings, mind intensive tasks, and other interpersonal interactions. High priority tasks should be done first. Some least important tasks can be done towards the end of the day.

Tip 2: Motion can drain your energy. Walking, driving, etc... can surely drain your energy. Instead of a work meeting, why not schedule a video call or a phone call? Not only can you get work done, but you also spent less energy. It saves you much time which can be allotted for other tasks.

Tip 3: The toughest time for those fasting can be the afternoon and early evening. This is the point where you experience the lowest energy. You can take an afternoon nap to regain energy (perfect time to do Dhikr while resting) This can recharge your senses just in time for the evening meal. If you can't take a short nap you can simply go to the washroom and wash your face. This helps you stay energized throughout the day.

List of Du'as

After Breaking Fast During Iftar

ذَهَبَ الظَّمَأُ وَابْتَلَّتِ الْعُرُوقُ وَثَبَتَ الْأَجْرُ إِنْ شَاءَ اللّٰهُ

Thirst has gone, the veins are quenched, and the reward is due, if Allah wills.

Transliteration

Dhahaba al-zama' wa abtalat al-'urooq wa thabata al-ajru in sha Allah

When You Break The Fast

اللَّهُمَّ لَكَ صُمْتُ وَ عَلَى رِزْقِكَ أَفْطَرْتُ وَ عَلَيْكَ تَوَكَّلْتُ

O Allah! For You I have fasted and upon your provision, I have broken my fast and I rely on you.

Transliteration

Allaahumma Laka S'umtu Wa A'laa Rizqika Aft'artuwa A'layka Tawawkkaltu

The Last 10 Nights Of Ramadan

اللَّهُمَّ إِنَّكَ عَفُوٌّ تُحِبُّ الْعَفْوَ فَاعْفُ عَنِّي

O Allah, you are Most forgiving, and you love forgiveness; so forgive me

Transliteration

Allahumma innaka 'afuwwun, tuhibbul-'afwa, fa'fu 'anni

The Most asked Dua of Prophet (PBUH)

رَبَّنَا آتِنَا فِي الدُّنْيَا حَسَنَةً وَفِي الآخِرَةِ حَسَنَةً وَقِنَا عَذَابَ النَّارِ

O Allah! Give us in this world that which is good and in the Hereafter that which is good, and save us from the punishment of the Fire.

Transliteration

Rabbana atina fid-dunya hasanatan, wa fil-akhirati hasanatan wa qina 'adhab-annar

Ramadan at a Glance

SUN	MON	TUE	WED	THUR	FRI	SAT

....

....

....

....

....

....

....

Good Deeds You Can Do This Ramadan

- ❏ "Constantly Do Dhikr"
- ❏ "Give From What You Love The Most"
- ❏ "Make Du'a - it's Ramadan The Month Of Forgiveness"
- ❏ "Always Smile"
- ❏ "Express Your Gratitude"
- ❏ "Sleep Less Pray More"
- ❏ "Share Your Knowledge!"
- ❏ "Forgive Others Around You"
- ❏ "Help Keep Your Environment Clean"
- ❏ "Donate To a Charity Of Your Choosing!"
- ❏ "Remember Your Parents and Family"
- ❏ "Invite Your Non-Muslim Friends and Neighbors To Join You In The Breaking Of Your Fast"

Note:

Feel free to use this journal as you want, Here are some examples

"Daily Schedule" Write "time" followed by your desired task

e.g

Morning:

08:00......Read Quran/ Work meeting

Evening:

18:00......Shopping time/ Go for a walk

Night:

21:00......Prepare for Taraweeh/ Zoom meeting

Then you have a prayer tracker, Dua of the day, etc...

For the "Daily reflection" section: Feel free to write any serious thought or consideration that you may have had, notes, ideas...

e.g

What did you learn?

Express your gratitude. What are you grateful for?

Quran reflections. What's in your Mind, Heart?

Acts of Kindness...

- ❑ Call a Friend
- ❑ Read Qur'an With Tafseer
- ❑ Feed a Fasting Person
- ❑ Show Appreciation
- ❑ Plant a Flower Or Tree
- ❑ Help Sick Animals To Find Homes
- ❑ Donate Books, Clothes, Toys To The Needy
- ❑ Seek a lot of Repentance (Istighfaar)
- ❑ Let Someone In-Line Go Ahead of You
- ❑ Buy Eid Clothes For An Orphan
- ❑ Serve At a Homeless Shelter
- ❑ Get Someone a Glass Of Water
- ❑ Make Iftar For a Family In Need
- ❑ Encourage Someone Who Needs It
- ❑ Buy Something New And Donate It Unused
- ❑ Leave Positive Sticky Notes To Your Co-workers
- ❑ Make Eid Cards For Your Friends, Family,
  and Even Strangers
- ❑
- ❑ ....
- ❑ ....
- ❑ ....
- ❑ ....
- ❑ ....
- ❑ ....
- ❑ ....
- ❑ ....

Reading Log

Day	Juz/Surah	Verse	To Verse

"Read! In The Name Of Your Lord, Who Has Created" [Quran 96:1]

Day	Juz/Surah	Verse	To Verse

Ramadan Day 1

Date ....

- [ ] Fajr
- [ ] Dhuhr
- [ ] Asr
- [ ] Maghrib
- [ ] Isha'a
- [ ] Taraweeh # ....

Daily Schedule

Time ☀ Morning

....

....

....

Time ☀ Afternoon

....

....

....

Time ⛅ Evening

....

....

....

Time 🌙 Night

....

....

....

Dua Of The Day

....

....

....

....

....

....

Today's Goals

- ○ ....
- ○ ....
- ○ ....

Sunnah Habits

- [ ] Morning Dhikr
- [ ] Exercise
- [ ] Eat Healthy
- [ ] Give to Charity
- [ ] Evening Dhikr
- [ ] 8 Glasses of Water
- [ ] Have A Balanced Varied Iftar

Iftar & Suhoor Meal Planner

Iftar	Suhoor
....	....
....	....
....	....

✔ To-Do List

....

....

....

On A Scale Of 1 To 5 How Did My Day Go?
① ② ③ ④ ⑤
How Can I Make Tomorrow Better?

....

💡 Daily Reflection

....

....

....

....

....

....

....

....

....

....

....

Ramadan Day 2

Date ....

☐ Fajr   ☐ Dhuhr
☐ Asr   ☐ Maghrib
☐ Isha'a   ☐ Taraweeh # ....

Daily Schedule

Time ☀ Morning

....
....
....

Time ☀ Afternoon

....
....
....

Time ☁ Evening

....
....
....

Time 🌙 Night

....
....
....

Dua Of The Day

....
....
....
....
....
....

Today's Goals

◯ ....
◯ ....
◯ ....

Sunnah Habits

☐ Morning Dhikr
☐ Exercise
☐ Eat Healthy
☐ Give to Charity
☐ Evening Dhikr
☐ 8 Glasses of Water
☐ Have A Balanced Varied Iftar

Iftar & Suhoor Meal Planner

Iftar	Suhoor

✓ To-Do List

On A Scale Of 1 To 5 How Did My Day Go?
① ② ③ ④ ⑤
How Can I Make Tomorrow Better?

💡 Daily Reflection

Ramadan Day 3

Date ....

☐ Fajr   ☐ Dhuhr
☐ Asr   ☐ Maghrib
☐ Isha'a   ☐ Taraweeh # ....

Daily Schedule

Time ☀ Morning

....
....
....

Time ☀ Afternoon

....
....
....

Time ⛅ Evening

....
....
....

Time 🌙 Night

....
....
....

Dua Of The Day

....
....
....
....
....
....

Today's Goals

○ ....
○ ....
○ ....

Sunnah Habits

☐ Morning Dhikr
☐ Exercise
☐ Eat Healthy
☐ Give to Charity
☐ Evening Dhikr
☐ 8 Glasses of Water
☐ Have A Balanced Varied Iftar

Iftar & Suhoor Meal Planner

Iftar	Suhoor
....	....
....	....
....	....

✓ To-Do List

....
....
....

On A Scale Of 1 To 5 How Did My Day Go?

① ② ③ ④ ⑤

How Can I Make Tomorrow Better?

....

💡 Daily Reflection

....
....
....
....
....
....
....
....
....
....
....
....

Ramadan Day 4

Date ....

☐ Fajr   ☐ Dhuhr
☐ Asr   ☐ Maghrib
☐ Isha'a ☐ Taraweeh # ....

Daily Schedule

Time ☼ Morning

....
....
....

Time ☼ Afternoon

....
....
....

Time ☁ Evening

....
....
....

Time ☾ Night

....
....
....

Dua Of The Day

....
....
....
....
....
....

Today's Goals

○ ....
○ ....
○ ....

Sunnah Habits

☐ Morning Dhikr
☐ Exercise
☐ Eat Healthy
☐ Give to Charity
☐ Evening Dhikr
☐ 8 Glasses of Water
☐ Have A Balanced Varied Iftar

Iftar & Suhoor Meal Planner

Iftar	Suhoor

✓ To-Do List

....
....
....

On A Scale Of 1 To 5 How Did My Day Go?

① ② ③ ④ ⑤

How Can I Make Tomorrow Better?

....

💡 Daily Reflection

....
....
....
....
....
....
....
....
....
....
....

Ramadan Day 5

Date ....

☐ Fajr ☐ Dhuhr
☐ Asr ☐ Maghrib
☐ Isha'a ☐ Taraweeh # ....

Daily Schedule

Time ☀ Morning

....
....
....

Time ☀ Afternoon

....
....
....

Time ⛅ Evening

....
....
....

Time 🌙 Night

....
....
....

Dua Of The Day

....
....
....
....
....
....

Today's Goals

○ ....
○ ....
○ ....

Sunnah Habits

☐ Morning Dhikr
☐ Exercise
☐ Eat Healthy
☐ Give to Charity
☐ Evening Dhikr
☐ 8 Glasses of Water
☐ Have A Balanced Varied Iftar

Iftar & Suhoor Meal Planner

Iftar	Suhoor

✓ To-Do List

....

....

....

On A Scale Of 1 To 5 How Did My Day Go?

① ② ③ ④ ⑤

How Can I Make Tomorrow Better?

....

💡 Daily Reflection

....

....

....

....

....

....

....

....

....

....

Ramadan Day 6

Date ....

□ Fajr   □ Dhuhr
□ Asr   □ Maghrib
□ Isha'a   □ Taraweeh # ....

Daily Schedule

Time ☀ Morning

....

....

....

Time ☀ Afternoon

....

....

....

Time ⛅ Evening

....

....

Time 🌙 Night

....

....

....

Dua Of The Day

....

....

....

....

....

....

Today's Goals

○ ....

○ ....

○ ....

Sunnah Habits

□ Morning Dhikr
□ Exercise
□ Eat Healthy
□ Give to Charity
□ Evening Dhikr
□ 8 Glasses of Water
□ Have A Balanced Varied Iftar

Iftar & Suhoor Meal Planner

Iftar	Suhoor
....	....
....	....
....	....

✓ To-Do List

....

....

....

On A Scale Of 1 To 5 How Did My Day Go?

① ② ③ ④ ⑤

How Can I Make Tomorrow Better?

....

💡 Daily Reflection

....

....

....

....

....

....

....

....

....

....

Ramadan Day 7

Date ....

☐ Fajr   ☐ Dhuhr
☐ Asr   ☐ Maghrib
☐ Isha'a   ☐ Taraweeh # ....

Daily Schedule

Time ☀ Morning

....

....

....

Time ☀ Afternoon

....

....

....

Time ⛅ Evening

....

....

....

Time 🌙 Night

....

....

....

Dua Of The Day

....

....

....

....

....

....

Today's Goals

○ ....

○ ....

○ ....

Sunnah Habits

☐ Morning Dhikr
☐ Exercise
☐ Eat Healthy
☐ Give to Charity
☐ Evening Dhikr
☐ 8 Glasses of Water
☐ Have A Balanced Varied Iftar

Iftar & Suhoor Meal Planner

Iftar	Suhoor
....	....
....	....
....	....

✓ To-Do List

....

....

....

On A Scale Of 1 To 5 How Did My Day Go?
① ② ③ ④ ⑤
How Can I Make Tomorrow Better?

....

💡 Daily Reflection

....

....

....

....

....

....

....

....

....

....

Ramadan Day 8

Date ....

☐ Fajr   ☐ Dhuhr
☐ Asr   ☐ Maghrib
☐ Isha'a   ☐ Taraweeh # ....

Daily Schedule

Time ☀ Morning

....

....

....

Time 😎 Afternoon

....

....

Time ⛅ Evening

....

....

....

Time 🌙 Night

....

....

....

Dua Of The Day

....
....
....
....
....
....
....

Today's Goals

○ ....
○ ....
○ ....

Sunnah Habits

☐ Morning Dhikr
☐ Exercise
☐ Eat Healthy
☐ Give to Charity
☐ Evening Dhikr
☐ 8 Glasses of Water
☐ Have A Balanced Varied Iftar

Iftar & Suhoor Meal Planner

Iftar	Suhoor
....	....
....	....
....	....

✓ To-Do List

....

....

....

On A Scale Of 1 To 5 How Did My Day Go?

① ② ③ ④ ⑤

How Can I Make Tomorrow Better?

....

💡 Daily Reflection

....

....

....

....

....

....

....

....

....

....

....

Ramadan Day 9

Date ....

☐ Fajr ☐ Dhuhr
☐ Asr ☐ Maghrib
☐ Isha'a ☐ Taraweeh # ......

Daily Schedule

Time ☀ Morning

....
....
....

Time ☀ Afternoon

....
....
....

Time ⛅ Evening

....
....
....

Time 🌙 Night

....
....
....

Dua Of The Day

....
....
....
....
....

Today's Goals

○ ....
○ ....
○ ....

Sunnah Habits

☐ Morning Dhikr
☐ Exercise
☐ Eat Healthy
☐ Give to Charity
☐ Evening Dhikr
☐ 8 Glasses of Water
☐ Have A Balanced Varied Iftar

Iftar & Suhoor Meal Planner

Iftar	Suhoor

✓ To-Do List

....

....

....

On A Scale Of 1 To 5 How Did My Day Go?
① ② ③ ④ ⑤
How Can I Make Tomorrow Better?

....

💡 Daily Reflection

....

....

....

....

....

....

....

....

....

....

....

....

Ramadan Day 10

Date ....

☐ Fajr   ☐ Dhuhr
☐ Asr   ☐ Maghrib
☐ Isha'a ☐ Taraweeh # ....

Daily Schedule

Time ☀ Morning

....
....
....

Time 😎 Afternoon

....
....

Time ⛅ Evening

....
....
....

Time 🌙 Night

....
....
....

Dua Of The Day

....
....
....
....
....
....

Today's Goals

○ ....
○ ....
○ ....

Sunnah Habits

☐ Morning Dhikr
☐ Exercise
☐ Eat Healthy
☐ Give to Charity
☐ Evening Dhikr
☐ 8 Glasses of Water
☐ Have A Balanced Varied Iftar

Iftar & Suhoor Meal Planner

Iftar	Suhoor

✓ To-Do List

On A Scale Of 1 To 5 How Did My Day Go?
① ② ③ ④ ⑤
How Can I Make Tomorrow Better?

💡 Daily Reflection

Ramadan Day 11

Date ....

☐ Fajr   ☐ Dhuhr
☐ Asr   ☐ Maghrib
☐ Isha'a   ☐ Taraweeh # ....

Daily Schedule

Time ☀ Morning

....
....
....

Time ☀ Afternoon

....
....

Time ⛅ Evening

....
....

Time 🌙 Night

....
....

Dua Of The Day

....
....
....
....
....

Today's Goals

○ ....
○ ....
○ ....

Sunnah Habits

☐ Morning Dhikr
☐ Exercise
☐ Eat Healthy
☐ Give to Charity
☐ Evening Dhikr
☐ 8 Glasses of Water
☐ Have A Balanced Varied Iftar

Iftar & Suhoor Meal Planner

Iftar	Suhoor
....	....
....	....
....	....

✓ To-Do List

....

....

....

On A Scale Of 1 To 5 How Did My Day Go?

① ② ③ ④ ⑤

How Can I Make Tomorrow Better?

....

💡 Daily Reflection

....

....

....

....

....

....

....

....

....

....

....

....

Ramadan Day 12

Date ....

☐ Fajr   ☐ Dhuhr
☐ Asr   ☐ Maghrib
☐ Isha'a   ☐ Taraweeh # ....

Daily Schedule

Time ☀ Morning

....

....

....

Time ☀ Afternoon

....

....

....

Time ⛅ Evening

....

....

....

Time 🌙 Night

....

....

Dua Of The Day

....

....

....

....

....

....

Today's Goals

○ ....

○ ....

○ ....

Sunnah Habits

☐ Morning Dhikr
☐ Exercise
☐ Eat Healthy
☐ Give to Charity
☐ Evening Dhikr
☐ 8 Glasses of Water
☐ Have A Balanced Varied Iftar

Iftar & Suhoor Meal Planner

Iftar	Suhoor
....	....
....	....
....	....

✓ To-Do List

....

....

....

On A Scale Of 1 To 5 How Did My Day Go?

① ② ③ ④ ⑤

How Can I Make Tomorrow Better?

....

....

💡 Daily Reflection

....

....

....

....

....

....

....

....

....

....

....

Ramadan Day 13

Date ....

Daily Schedule _____

Time ☀ Morning

....
....
....

Time ☀ Afternoon

....
....
....

Time ⛅ Evening

....
....
....

Time 🌙 Night

....
....
....

☐ Fajr   ☐ Dhuhr
☐ Asr   ☐ Maghrib
☐ Isha'a   ☐ Taraweeh # ....

Dua Of The Day

....
....
....
....
....
....

Today's Goals

◯ ....
◯ ....
◯ ....

Sunnah Habits

☐ Morning Dhikr
☐ Exercise
☐ Eat Healthy
☐ Give to Charity
☐ Evening Dhikr
☐ 8 Glasses of Water
☐ Have A Balanced Varied Iftar

Iftar & Suhoor Meal Planner

Iftar	Suhoor

✓ To-Do List

On A Scale Of 1 To 5 How Did My Day Go?

① ② ③ ④ ⑤

How Can I Make Tomorrow Better?

💡 Daily Reflection

Ramadan Day 14

Date ....

☐ Fajr   ☐ Dhuhr
☐ Asr   ☐ Maghrib
☐ Isha'a   ☐ Taraweeh #

Daily Schedule

Time ☀ Morning

....
....
....

Time 😎 Afternoon

....
....

Time ⛅ Evening

....
....
....

Time 🌙 Night

....
....
....

Dua Of The Day

....
....
....
....
....
....

Today's Goals

○ ....
○ ....
○ ....

Sunnah Habits

☐ Morning Dhikr
☐ Exercise
☐ Eat Healthy
☐ Give to Charity
☐ Evening Dhikr
☐ 8 Glasses of Water
☐ Have A Balanced Varied Iftar

Iftar & Suhoor Meal Planner

Iftar	Suhoor
....	....
....	....
....	....

✓ To-Do List

....

....

....

On A Scale Of 1 To 5 How Did My Day Go?
① ② ③ ④ ⑤
How Can I Make Tomorrow Better?

....

💡 Daily Reflection

....

....

....

....

....

....

....

....

....

....

Ramadan Day 15

Date ....

☐ Fajr   ☐ Dhuhr
☐ Asr   ☐ Maghrib
☐ Isha'a   ☐ Taraweeh # ....

Daily Schedule

Time ☀ Morning

....

....

....

Time ☀ Afternoon

....

....

....

Time ☁ Evening

....

....

....

Time 🌙 Night

....

....

Dua Of The Day

....

....

....

....

....

....

Today's Goals

◯ ....

◯ ....

◯ ....

Sunnah Habits

☐ Morning Dhikr
☐ Exercise
☐ Eat Healthy
☐ Give to Charity
☐ Evening Dhikr
☐ 8 Glasses of Water
☐ Have A Balanced Varied Iftar

Iftar & Suhoor Meal Planner

Iftar	Suhoor
....	....
....	....
....	....

✓ To-Do List

....

....

....

On A Scale Of 1 To 5 How Did My Day Go?
① ② ③ ④ ⑤
How Can I Make Tomorrow Better?

....

💡 Daily Reflection

....

....

....

....

....

....

....

....

....

....

....

....

Ramadan Day 16

Date ....

Daily Schedule

Time ☀ Morning
....
....
....

Time ☀ Afternoon
....
....
....

Time ⛅ Evening
....
....
....

Time 🌙 Night
....
....
....

☐ Fajr   ☐ Dhuhr
☐ Asr   ☐ Maghrib
☐ Isha'a   ☐ Taraweeh # ....

Dua Of The Day
....
....
....
....
....
....

Today's Goals
◯ ....
◯ ....
◯ ....

Sunnah Habits

☐ Morning Dhikr
☐ Exercise
☐ Eat Healthy
☐ Give to Charity
☐ Evening Dhikr
☐ 8 Glasses of Water
☐ Have A Balanced Varied Iftar

Iftar & Suhoor Meal Planner

Iftar	Suhoor

✓ To-Do List

....

....

....

On A Scale Of 1 To 5 How Did My Day Go?

① ② ③ ④ ⑤

How Can I Make Tomorrow Better?

....

💡 Daily Reflection

....

....

....

....

....

....

....

....

....

....

....

....

Ramadan Day 17

Date ....

☐ Fajr   ☐ Dhuhr
☐ Asr   ☐ Maghrib
☐ Isha'a   ☐ Taraweeh # ......

Daily Schedule

Time ☀ Morning

Dua Of The Day

....

....

....

Time ☀ Afternoon

....

....

Today's Goals

○ ....

....

○ ....

Time ☁ Evening

○ ....

....

....

Sunnah Habits

☐ Morning Dhikr
☐ Exercise
☐ Eat Healthy

Time 🌙 Night

☐ Give to Charity
☐ Evening Dhikr

....

☐ 8 Glasses of Water

....

☐ Have A Balanced Varied Iftar

Iftar & Suhoor Meal Planner

Iftar	Suhoor
....	....
....	....
....	....

✓ To-Do List

....

....

....

On A Scale Of 1 To 5 How Did My Day Go?

① ② ③ ④ ⑤

How Can I Make Tomorrow Better?

....

💡 Daily Reflection

....

....

....

....

....

....

....

....

....

....

....

Ramadan Day 18

Date ....

☐ Fajr ☐ Dhuhr
☐ Asr ☐ Maghrib
☐ Isha'a ☐ Taraweeh # ....

Daily Schedule

Time ☀ Morning

....
....
....

Time 😎 Afternoon

....
....
....

Time ⛅ Evening

....
....
....

Time 🌙 Night

....
....
....

Dua Of The Day

....
....
....
....
....
....

Today's Goals

○ ....
○ ....
○ ....

Sunnah Habits

☐ Morning Dhikr
☐ Exercise
☐ Eat Healthy
☐ Give to Charity
☐ Evening Dhikr
☐ 8 Glasses of Water
☐ Have A Balanced Varied Iftar

Iftar & Suhoor Meal Planner

Iftar	Suhoor

✓ To-Do List

....

....

....

On A Scale Of 1 To 5 How Did My Day Go?
① ② ③ ④ ⑤
How Can I Make Tomorrow Better?

....

💡 Daily Reflection

....

....

....

....

....

....

....

....

....

....

....

Ramadan Day 19

Date ....

☐ Fajr   ☐ Dhuhr
☐ Asr   ☐ Maghrib
☐ Isha'a   ☐ Taraweeh # ......

Daily Schedule

Time ☼ Morning

....
....
....

Time ☼ Afternoon

....
....
....

Time ⛅ Evening

....
....
....

Time 🌙 Night

....
....
....

Dua Of The Day

....
....
....
....
....
....
....
....

Today's Goals

○ ....
○ ....
○ ....

Sunnah Habits

☐ Morning Dhikr
☐ Exercise
☐ Eat Healthy
☐ Give to Charity
☐ Evening Dhikr
☐ 8 Glasses of Water
☐ Have A Balanced Varied Iftar

Iftar & Suhoor Meal Planner

Iftar	Suhoor
....	....
....	....
....	....

✓ To-Do List

....
....
....

On A Scale Of 1 To 5 How Did My Day Go?

① ② ③ ④ ⑤

How Can I Make Tomorrow Better?

....

💡 Daily Reflection

....
....
....
....
....
....
....
....
....
....

Ramadan Day 20

Date ....

☐ Fajr   ☐ Dhuhr
☐ Asr   ☐ Maghrib
☐ Isha'a ☐ Taraweeh # ......

Daily Schedule

Time ☀ Morning

....
....
....

Dua Of The Day

....
....
....
....
....

Time ☀ Afternoon

....
....
....

Today's Goals

○ ....
○ ....
○ ....

Time ⛅ Evening

....
....

Sunnah Habits

Time 🌙 Night

☐ Morning Dhikr
☐ Exercise
☐ Eat Healthy
☐ Give to Charity
☐ Evening Dhikr
☐ 8 Glasses of Water
☐ Have A Balanced Varied Iftar

Iftar & Suhoor Meal Planner

Iftar	Suhoor
....	....
....	....
....	....

✓ To-Do List

....

....

....

On A Scale Of 1 To 5 How Did My Day Go?
① ② ③ ④ ⑤
How Can I Make Tomorrow Better?

....

💡 Daily Reflection

....

....

....

....

....

....

....

....

....

....

....

Ramadan Day 21

Date ....

☐ Fajr   ☐ Dhuhr
☐ Asr   ☐ Maghrib
☐ Isha'a   ☐ Taraweeh # ....

Daily Schedule

Time ☼ Morning

....

....

....

Time ☼ Afternoon

....

....

....

Time ☁ Evening

....

....

....

Time 🌙 Night

....

....

....

Dua Of The Day

....

....

....

....

....

....

Today's Goals

○ ....

○ ....

○ ....

Sunnah Habits

☐ Morning Dhikr
☐ Exercise
☐ Eat Healthy
☐ Give to Charity
☐ Evening Dhikr
☐ 8 Glasses of Water
☐ Have A Balanced Varied Iftar

Iftar & Suhoor Meal Planner

Iftar	Suhoor
......	......
......	......
......	......

✓ To-Do List

....

....

....

On A Scale Of 1 To 5 How Did My Day Go?

① ② ③ ④ ⑤

How Can I Make Tomorrow Better?

....

💡 Daily Reflection

....

....

....

....

....

....

....

....

....

....

Ramadan Day 22

Date ....

☐ Fajr   ☐ Dhuhr
☐ Asr   ☐ Maghrib
☐ Isha'a   ☐ Taraweeh # ......

Daily Schedule

Time ☼ Morning

....

....

....

Time 😎 Afternoon

....

....

....

Time ⛅ Evening

....

....

....

Time 🌙 Night

....

....

....

Dua Of The Day

....

....

....

....

....

....

Today's Goals

○ ....

○ ....

○ ....

Sunnah Habits

☐ Morning Dhikr
☐ Exercise
☐ Eat Healthy
☐ Give to Charity
☐ Evening Dhikr
☐ 8 Glasses of Water
☐ Have A Balanced Varied Iftar

Iftar & Suhoor Meal Planner

Iftar	Suhoor
....	....
....	....
....	....

✓ To-Do List

....

....

....

On A Scale Of 1 To 5 How Did My Day Go?
① ② ③ ④ ⑤
How Can I Make Tomorrow Better?

....

💡 Daily Reflection

....

....

....

....

....

....

....

....

....

....

....

Ramadan Day 23

Date ....

- [ ] Fajr
- [ ] Dhuhr
- [ ] Asr
- [ ] Maghrib
- [ ] Isha'a
- [ ] Taraweeh # ....

Daily Schedule

Time ☼ Morning

....
....
....

Time ☼ Afternoon

....
....
....

Time ☁ Evening

....
....
....

Time ☾ Night

....
....
....

Dua Of The Day

....
....
....
....
....

Today's Goals

- ◯ ....
- ◯ ....
- ◯ ....

Sunnah Habits

- [ ] Morning Dhikr
- [ ] Exercise
- [ ] Eat Healthy
- [ ] Give to Charity
- [ ] Evening Dhikr
- [ ] 8 Glasses of Water
- [ ] Have A Balanced Varied Iftar

Iftar & Suhoor Meal Planner

Iftar	Suhoor

✓ To-Do List

....

....

....

On A Scale Of 1 To 5 How Did My Day Go?
① ② ③ ④ ⑤
How Can I Make Tomorrow Better?

....

💡 Daily Reflection

....

....

....

....

....

....

....

....

....

....

....

Ramadan Day 24

Date ....

☐ Fajr   ☐ Dhuhr
☐ Asr   ☐ Maghrib
☐ Isha'a ☐ Taraweeh # ....

Daily Schedule

Time ☀ Morning

....
....
....

Time 😎 Afternoon

....
....

Time ⛅ Evening

....
....
....

Time 🌙 Night

....
....
....

Dua Of The Day

Today's Goals

○
○
○

Sunnah Habits

☐ Morning Dhikr
☐ Exercise
☐ Eat Healthy
☐ Give to Charity
☐ Evening Dhikr
☐ 8 Glasses of Water
☐ Have A Balanced Varied Iftar

Iftar & Suhoor Meal Planner

Iftar	Suhoor

✓ To-Do List

....

....

....

On A Scale Of 1 To 5 How Did My Day Go?
① ② ③ ④ ⑤
How Can I Make Tomorrow Better?

....

💡 Daily Reflection

....

....

....

....

....

....

....

....

....

....

Ramadan Day 25

Date ....

☐ Fajr   ☐ Dhuhr
☐ Asr   ☐ Maghrib
☐ Isha'a   ☐ Taraweeh # ....

Daily Schedule

Time ☼ Morning

....
....
....

Time ☼ Afternoon

....
....
....

Time ⛅ Evening

....
....
....

Time 🌙 Night

....
....
....

Dua Of The Day

....
....
....
....
....
....

Today's Goals

○ ....
○ ....
○ ....

Sunnah Habits

☐ Morning Dhikr
☐ Exercise
☐ Eat Healthy
☐ Give to Charity
☐ Evening Dhikr
☐ 8 Glasses of Water
☐ Have A Balanced Varied Iftar

Iftar & Suhoor Meal Planner

Iftar	Suhoor
....	....
....	....
....	....
....	....

✓ To-Do List

....
....
....

On A Scale Of 1 To 5 How Did My Day Go?

① ② ③ ④ ⑤

How Can I Make Tomorrow Better?

....

💡 Daily Reflection

....
....
....
....
....
....
....
....
....
....
....

Ramadan Day 26

Date ....

☐ Fajr ☐ Dhuhr
☐ Asr ☐ Maghrib
☐ Isha'a ☐ Taraweeh # ....

Daily Schedule

Time ☀ Morning

....

....

....

Time ☀ Afternoon

....

....

....

Time ☁ Evening

....

....

....

Time 🌙 Night

....

....

....

Dua Of The Day

....

....

....

....

....

....

Today's Goals

○ ....

○ ....

○ ....

Sunnah Habits

☐ Morning Dhikr
☐ Exercise
☐ Eat Healthy
☐ Give to Charity
☐ Evening Dhikr
☐ 8 Glasses of Water
☐ Have A Balanced Varied Iftar

Iftar & Suhoor Meal Planner

Iftar	Suhoor
....	....
....	....
....	....

✓ To-Do List

....

....

....

On A Scale Of 1 To 5 How Did My Day Go?

① ② ③ ④ ⑤

How Can I Make Tomorrow Better?

....

💡 Daily Reflection

....

....

....

....

....

....

....

....

....

....

....

Ramadan Day 27

Date ....

Daily Schedule

Time ☼ Morning

....

....

....

Time ☼ Afternoon

....

....

....

Time ⛅ Evening

....

....

....

Time 🌙 Night

....

....

....

☐ Fajr   ☐ Dhuhr
☐ Asr   ☐ Maghrib
☐ Isha'a   ☐ Taraweeh # .....

Dua Of The Day

....

....

....

....

....

....

Today's Goals

◯ ....

◯ ....

◯ ....

Sunnah Habits

☐ Morning Dhikr
☐ Exercise
☐ Eat Healthy
☐ Give to Charity
☐ Evening Dhikr
☐ 8 Glasses of Water
☐ Have A Balanced Varied Iftar

Iftar & Suhoor Meal Planner

Iftar	Suhoor
....	....
....	....
....	....

✓ To-Do List

....

....

....

On A Scale Of 1 To 5 How Did My Day Go?

① ② ③ ④ ⑤

How Can I Make Tomorrow Better?

....

💡 Daily Reflection

....

....

....

....

....

....

....

....

....

....

Ramadan Day 28

Date ....

☐ Fajr   ☐ Dhuhr
☐ Asr   ☐ Maghrib
☐ Isha'a   ☐ Taraweeh # ......

Daily Schedule

Time ☀ Morning

....
....
....

Time 😎 Afternoon

....
....

Time ⛅ Evening

....

Time 🌙 Night

....
....

Dua Of The Day

....
....
....
....
....
....

Today's Goals

○ ....
○ ....
○ ....

Sunnah Habits

☐ Morning Dhikr
☐ Exercise
☐ Eat Healthy
☐ Give to Charity
☐ Evening Dhikr
☐ 8 Glasses of Water
☐ Have A Balanced Varied Iftar

Iftar & Suhoor Meal Planner

Iftar	Suhoor
....	....
....	....
....	....

✓ To-Do List

....

....

....

On A Scale Of 1 To 5 How Did My Day Go?
① ② ③ ④ ⑤
How Can I Make Tomorrow Better?

....

💡 Daily Reflection

....

....

....

....

....

....

....

....

....

....

....

Ramadan Day 29

Date ....

☐ Fajr   ☐ Dhuhr
☐ Asr   ☐ Maghrib
☐ Isha'a ☐ Taraweeh # ......

Daily Schedule

Time ☀ Morning

....
....
....

Time ☀ Afternoon

....
....
....

Time ⛅ Evening

....
....
....

Time 🌙 Night

....
....

Dua Of The Day

....
....
....
....
....
....
....

Today's Goals

○ ....
○ ....
○ ....

Sunnah Habits

☐ Morning Dhikr
☐ Exercise
☐ Eat Healthy
☐ Give to Charity
☐ Evening Dhikr
☐ 8 Glasses of Water
☐ Have A Balanced Varied Iftar

Iftar & Suhoor Meal Planner

Iftar	Suhoor
....	....
....	....
....	....

✓ To-Do List

....

....

....

On A Scale Of 1 To 5 How Did My Day Go?

① ② ③ ④ ⑤

How Can I Make Tomorrow Better?

....

💡 Daily Reflection

....

....

....

....

....

....

....

....

....

....

....

Ramadan Day 30

Date ....

☐ Fajr   ☐ Dhuhr
☐ Asr   ☐ Maghrib
☐ Isha'a   ☐ Taraweeh # ....

Daily Schedule

Time ☀ Morning

Dua Of The Day

....

....

....

....

Time 😎 Afternoon

Today's Goals

○ ....

○ ....

○ ....

Time ⛅ Evening

Sunnah Habits

☐ Morning Dhikr
☐ Exercise
☐ Eat Healthy
☐ Give to Charity
☐ Evening Dhikr
☐ 8 Glasses of Water
☐ Have A Balanced Varied Iftar

Time 🌙 Night

Iftar & Suhoor Meal Planner

Iftar	Suhoor

✓ To-Do List

....

....

....

On A Scale Of 1 To 5 How Did My Day Go?
① ② ③ ④ ⑤
How Can I Make Tomorrow Better?

....

💡 Daily Reflection

....

....

....

....

....

....

....

....

....

....

....

Laylat al-Qadr Plans (the Night of Decree)

"The Night of Decree is better than a thousand months,"

(Qur'an, 97:3)

Estimated Date

....

Goals for Laylat al-Qadr

○ ....   ○ ....
○ ....   ○ ....
○ ....   ○ ....

Duas to Make	Surahs to Recite

To-Do List

....

....

....

....

....

Post Ramadan Reflections

Write down what are Habits/Activities you will start, stop, change, and continue after Ramadan with respect to your worship and character.

Habits to Start	Habits to Stop
Habits to Change	**Habits to Continue**

Habits are an important force that our brains actually cling to because essentially they create neurological cravings where a certain behavior is rewarded by the release of "pleasure" chemicals in the brain. Your life today is the sum of your habits whether you do your prayer, take time for dhikr, appreciate Allah (SWT) for the blessings in your life, pick up and read the Quran, face your co-workers with a cheerful face, etc... Being conscious of Allah can help you live a fulfilled life finding happiness in every area of your life.

Eid al Fitr is the day of celebration on completing sawm in the month of Ramadan. the festival commences on the 1st of Shawwal. Some Muslims observe six days of fasting during Shawwāl beginning the day after Eid ul-Fitr. It's not required to fast six days continuously without any interruption. One can fast according to convenience any time during the month. These six days of fasting together with the Ramadan fasts are equivalent to fasting all year round.

☐ Day 1   ☐ Day 2   ☐ Day 3

☐ Day 4   ☐ Day 5   ☐ Day 6

Eid Checklist

☐ Shop Eid Outfit
☐ Pay Zakat Al Fitr
☐ Plan Eid (home, decor...)
☐ Write Eid Cards
☐ Prepare Eid Menu
☐ Wrap Eid Gifts
☐ ....
☐ ....
☐ ....
☐ ....
☐ ....
☐ ....
☐ ....
☐ ....
☐ ....
☐ ....
☐ ....

Made in United States
North Haven, CT
27 February 2023

33285099R00050